THE C

FOR

CUMBERLAND PRESBYTERIANS

APPROVED JUNE 2008

BY THE

GENERAL ASSEMBLY
OF THE CUMBERLAND PRESBYTERIAN CHURCH

May 2012

Cumberland Presbyterian Resources
8207 Traditional Place
Cordova (Memphis), Tennessee 38016

Prepared and published by the Discipleship Ministry Team of the Ministry Council of the Cumberland Presbyterian Church.

Funded, in part, by your contributions to Our United Outreach.

First Edition, First Printing, May 2012

ISBN-13: 978-0615638805
ISBN-10: 0615638805

OUR UNITED OUTREACH
Made Possible In Part By Your Tithe To Our United Outreach

THE CATECHISM

FOR

CUMBERLAND PRESBYTERIANS

CONTENTS

WHY A CATECHISM?

After I made my profession of faith at around eight years old, my parents gave a copy of the 1883 *Confession of Faith* to me[1]. I took to reading bits and pieces of it before I went to sleep at night. I didn't understand much of what I read, but I liked the smell when I opened the dark blue covers, and the feel of the small, slick pages. That book was a sign to me of who I was and who I wanted to become, a believer who belonged to that part of the church known as Cumberland Presbyterians.

The shorter Catechism was a part of that 1883 Confession, and was used as a tool to pass on the faith to growing believers. The Catechism consisted of questions asked by an instructor, and answers memorized by the student on everything from the nature of the Trinity to the meaning of the Lord's Prayer. However, Catechisms began to fall out of favor at the turn of the twentieth century. The language was outdated and often difficult for children to understand. Church educators began to call into question the effectiveness of memorizing rote answers to theological questions. And naturally, as the primary means of instruction, catechisms gave the impression that belief was mainly a matter of thinking right rather than living faithfully.

But now, catechetical instruction is making something of a comeback. We have discovered that we may need what catechisms offer, namely, a rich vocabulary for expressing our faith and a theological way of looking at the world. With these goals in mind, a new Catechism has been produced that reflects central and unique themes of the 1984 Confession of Faith. In 2004, the General Assembly approved this Catechism for study. It has since been sent to every session clerk of every congregation in the denomination.

---

[1] The full text of the 1883 Catechism can be found beginning on page 15 of this volume.

No one wants to return to the days when children were expected to memorize the long and sometimes tedious answers to confusing questions. But we do want our children to understand some key concepts, such as saving faith and the one covenant of grace. We also want to equip them with a peculiarly Christian way of seeing the world that is redemptively different from the viewpoint of, let's say, Madison Avenue. Handled appropriately, a Catechism can help shape us into people who think and act as Christians are called to think and act.

Up the road from Greeneville at the New Bethel CP Church, a teacher gathers her young students on Sunday morning to teach the Catechism. I wonder what questions will become their favorites. Perhaps 8: Does God want people to perish? No, it is not God's desire that anyone should perish. Or, how about 41. Where is the Spirit now? The Spirit is everywhere, working to help people know the love of God in Jesus Christ. Then again, it could be 57: What is the purpose of the church? The purpose of the church is to worship God and share God's love with the world. I can't imagine anything but good coming from the tucking away of these and similar questions in the minds of those budding believers.

Written by James W. Lively, Greeneville, TN, member of the Catechism Committee. Reprinted from THE CUMBERLAND PRESBYTERIAN, July 2004.

THE CATECHISM

1. Who is God?

God is the one living, active Creator of all that is, seen and unseen.

2. Who are we?

We are a part of God's creation, made in God's own image.

3. How do we know God?

God reveals himself to us as Father, Son, and Holy Spirit.

4. Is God male or female?

No. God does not have a body. Therefore, God is neither male nor female.

5. What is God like?

- God is strong and wise.
- God does what is good and right.
- God speaks the truth.
- God surrounds us always and everywhere.
- God lives forever.
- God never changes.
- Above all, God is love.

6. How do we know God is love?

We know God is love because God gave the Son for us. Everyone who trusts the Son belongs to God's family, and will not perish, but will live with God now and forever.

7. What does it mean to perish?

To perish is to be separated from God forever, to be denied the joy, peace, and purpose that come from living with God.

8. Does God want people to perish?

> No. It is not God's desire that anyone should perish.

9. How do we learn about God's love?

> We learn about God's love from the Bible; through God's people, the church; in the events of nature and history; and in many other ways; but most clearly through Jesus Christ.

10. What is the Bible?

> The Bible is the written record of God's mighty acts.

11. What are some of God's mighty acts in the Bible?

> The Bible tells that, through grace, God
> - created the world and everything in it
> - called a special people to be servants in the world
> - judges sinful humanity
> - became a human being in Jesus Christ to save the world
> - continues to love and care for creation throughout time
> - promises at last to bring believers into God's eternal presence.

12. What is grace?

> Grace is God's decision to create us, to care for us, and to claim us as children even though we do not deserve it. God gives all people the freedom to respond to God's grace.

13. How should we respond to God's grace?

> The proper response to grace is to admit our need for God, to trust God and obey God's will, and to give thanks for all the wonderful things God has done and is doing.

14. How do we respond to God's grace?

> All people rebel against God's grace. We try to live as if we do not need God. We ignore who the loving God wants us to be.

15. What do we call our attempt to live without God?

Our attempt to live without God is called sin.

16. What happens as the result of sin?

Our relationships with God and others become broken. We get trapped in hurtful words, attitudes, and actions, and we cannot free ourselves.

17. Does God stop loving us when we sin?

No. God does not reject us even when we sin.

18. How does God deal with our sin?

God calls us back from our broken relationships. God judges us and forgives us.

19. How does God judge us?

God forces us to face our sin–the harm we do to God, one another, and ourselves.

20. How does God forgive us?

God starts over with us. God renews the relationship with us, not counting our sins against us.

21. What do we call our relationship to God?

We call our relationship to God a covenant. God began the covenant long ago, has renewed it many times throughout the centuries, and has fulfilled it in the life, death, and resurrection of Jesus Christ. Still today, God upholds this covenant of grace.

22. What does God promise to do in the covenant?

God promises to bless us and to make us a blessing to all the peoples of the earth. We become a blessing as God uses us to share the knowledge and promises of God with others.

23. What do we promise to do in the covenant?

> We promise to trust and obey God.

24. What has God given us to help us keep the covenant?

> One of God's gifts to us in keeping the covenant is the Ten Commandments.

25. How do the Ten Commandments help us?

> The Ten Commandments tell us how to love and obey God.
> - You shall worship no other gods.
> - You shall not make any idols to worship.
> - You shall not use God's name in a disrespectful way.
> - Keep the Sabbath day holy as a time to rest and to worship God.

The Ten Commandments also tell us how to love and respect each other.

> - Honor your father and mother.
> - You shall not murder.
> - You shall not commit adultery.
> - You shall not steal.
> - You shall not lie about your neighbor.
> - You shall not envy what other people have.

26. Have people through the ages kept the covenant?

> They have not, and neither do we.

27. What did God do about our disobedience?

> In Jesus Christ, God renewed the covenant of grace so that all the world might know God's love.

28. What does the name *Jesus* mean?

> The name *Jesus* means Savior.

29. What does the title *Christ* mean?

The title *Christ* means the Messiah, the anointed one chosen by God.

30. Was Jesus like other human beings?

Yes and no. He was fully human and also fully God. He was tempted as we are, but he did not sin.

31. How did Jesus show God's love for us while he lived on earth?

- He called people to turn from sin.
- He prayed for others.
- He healed the sick.
- He fed the hungry.
- He forgave sinners.
- He welcomed all people.
- He taught about God's grace.

32. What happened to Jesus at the end of his life?

Jesus was killed for human sin. People crucified him on a cross.

33. What does the cross tell us about ourselves?

The cross tells us that our rebellion against God is serious.

34. What does the cross tell us about God?

The cross tells us that God's grace is greater than our sin. Human beings intended the cross for evil, but God used it for good.

35. How did God turn the cross into something good?

God used the death and resurrection of Jesus as the means by which sins are forgiven, once and for all people everywhere.

36. Did God make Jesus suffer and die on the cross?

No. Jesus was willing to die for our sake.

37. What happened after Jesus' death?

On the third day after being crucified, Jesus was raised from the dead. He appeared first to women at the tomb, and then to many other witnesses, including his closest disciples.

38. Why do we call Jesus "Lord"?

We call him Lord because he rules over all and makes sure that nothing will ever separate us from God's love.

39. In what other way do we know God?

We also know God as Holy Spirit.

40. On what day did the Holy Spirit come on the first followers of Jesus?

On the day of Pentecost. At Pentecost, the disciples received power from the Holy Spirit to share God's love with all people.

41. Where is the Spirit now?

The Spirit is everywhere, working to help people know the love of God in Jesus Christ.

42. What does the Spirit do?

The Spirit calls all people to trust in Jesus Christ and to live in the covenant of grace.

43. How does the Spirit speak to people?

The Spirit speaks to people through the Bible, the church, the witness of believers, and in ways beyond human understanding.

44. What does it mean *to be saved*?

To be saved means to live in the covenant of grace, to accept Jesus Christ as Lord and Savior, and to promise, with the help of the Spirit, to follow God's will. Whoever is willing to be saved may be saved, but not without the help of the Spirit.

45. What are some of the words we use to describe the gift of salvation?

We may use these words and phrases to describe the gift of salvation: repentance, confession, saving faith, justification, regeneration, adoption, sanctification, growth in grace, preservation of believers, and Christian assurance.

46. What does *repentance* mean?

Repentance means to turn away from words, attitudes, and actions that hurt God and others and to turn toward God. Repentance also means to say, "I'm sorry."

47. What does *confession* mean?

Confession means admitting our sin and asking God to forgive us. We also seek to repair the harm we have done to others as much as we can.

48. What does *saving faith* mean?

Saving faith means trusting in God's grace for our salvation instead of trusting in our own efforts.

49. What does *justification* mean?

Justification means God acts to restore a relationship with us, even though we are sinners.

50. What does *regeneration* mean?

Regeneration means to be made new in the sight of God. Other words for regeneration are recreated, born again, or born from above.

51. What does *adoption* mean?

Adoption means being accepted into God's family, sinful people though we are.

52. What does *sanctification* mean?

Sanctification means being set apart. God does not make us better than or more important than other people. Instead, God helps us become people who love God and whose actions reflect that love.

53. How does growth in grace occur?

We grow in grace and knowledge of Jesus Christ as we worship God, study the Bible, interact with other believers, and serve those in need. God calls us to grow in grace as long as we live.

54. What is the church's teaching about the preservation of believers?

The preservation of believers reminds us that God is always faithful, even though we are not. God will fulfill the covenant of grace and bring us to eternal life.

55. What is Christian assurance?

Christian assurance is the confidence we gain that God will not leave or forsake us, in life or in death. As we live the Christian life, our assurance deepens.

56. What are the people called who are saved by the Spirit?

They are called by the name of Jesus Christ—Christians. Christians make up the church, the people from every time and every place who put their trust in Jesus Christ as Lord and Savior.

57. What is the purpose of the church?

The purpose of the church is to worship God and to share God's love with the world.

58. What does the church do in worship?

The church gathers in the presence of the living God to celebrate God's wonderful deeds.

59. What actions are included in Christian worship?

- singing praise to God
- confessing our sin and receiving God's forgiveness
- reading from the Bible
- proclaiming the good news of Jesus Christ
- listening for God's word to us
- celebrating the sacraments
- praying for ourselves and others
- committing ourselves to God—our time, talent, and money
- receiving God's blessing

60. What does God do in worship?

In worship, God nourishes and strengthens the church through the preaching of the Word and the celebration of the sacraments.

61. What are the sacraments?

The sacraments are signs of God's covenant of grace with us. God not only tells us that we are loved; through the sacraments, God shows us that we are loved.

62. What sacraments do we celebrate?

We celebrate two sacraments: baptism and the Lord's supper.

63. What does baptism signify?

In baptism, God claims us as God's own people. In the act of baptism, water is a sign that our sins are forgiven and that we have received the outpouring of the Holy Spirit.

64. Do we have to be baptized in order to be saved?

No. God shows us through baptism that we belong to God's family. Therefore, baptism is a gift that believers gladly receive for themselves and their children.

65. What happens in the Lord's supper?

As we eat the bread and drink from the cup, we are united with Jesus Christ in his death and resurrection, with one another, and with Christians of every generation. Christ meets us at the communion table and gives us strength to be his faithful followers.

66. Who is invited to the Lord's supper?

Christ welcomes all who are part of the covenant community and are committed to the Christian life to eat this meal.

67. How do the sacraments strengthen the church?

The sacraments strengthen the church to share the love of Jesus Christ with all people, including those outside the church.

68. How do we share the love of God in Jesus Christ?

We share the love of God in Jesus Christ by telling others the good news about Jesus and by helping those who suffer and are oppressed.

69. Why do we care about people outside the church?

We care for people outside the church because they were created in God's image and because Christ gave his life for all of us.

70. Do we expect the church to grow in numbers?

Yes. As we share the good news of Jesus Christ, others come to believe in him and want to become a part of God's covenant family. We do all we can to welcome new believers as our brothers and sisters in Christ.

71. How do Christians relate to the world?

Christians are responsible to live out their faith at home and in the world by creatively using their skills and energies in every relationship. Christians are also called to be good stewards of the earth's resources for the good of all.

72. Do we face conflict as we seek to live faithful lives?

Yes. God calls us to be loving and just in all our relationships, to stand up especially for those who are weak and oppressed. This witness often puts us in conflict with those who do not seek the will of God.

73. What prayer did Jesus give to those who attempt to be his witnesses?

The Lord's Prayer:

Our Father in Heaven, hallowed be your name,
Your kingdom come, Your will be done, on earth as in heaven.
Give us today our daily bread.
Forgive us our sins as we forgive those who sin against us.
Save us from the time of trial, and deliver us from evil.
For the kingdom, the power, and the glory
are yours now and forever. Amen.

74. Why do we start the prayer with "Our Father in heaven"?

Because Jesus taught us that God is even better than the best parents on earth. When we pray, God comes to us from beyond this world to listen earnestly to our prayers.

75. What do we mean by *hallowed be your name*?

We are saying that God's name is holy and asking that people everywhere will come to honor God and not misuse God's name.

76. Why do we ask *your kingdom come, your will be done, on earth as in heaven*?

We expect God to transform this earth into a place where God's love rules, just as in heaven. We yield our wills to God's will so that we can be instruments of God's love.

77. What are we saying when we pray *give us today our daily bread*?

We are acknowledging that God alone provides what we need to live, and that everything we receive daily is a gift from God.

78. How do we understand the phrase *forgive our sins, as we forgive those who sin against us*?

Knowing God's grace for sinners, we admit what we have done wrong, trusting that God will forgive us. Likewise, we ask for strength to forgive those who have hurt us.

79. What do we mean when we pray *save us from the time of trial and deliver us from evil*?

We ask God's help to keep us free from destructive words, attitudes, and actions; and if we should be threatened by people or powers, we ask God to deliver us from harm.

80. What are we doing when we pray *for the kingdom and the power and the glory are yours now and forever*?

We are celebrating that the God of grace is stronger than evil. Although God's will sometimes appears to be defeated, the kingdoms of this world shall become the kingdom of Christ and he shall reign forever and ever.

81. Why do we end the prayer with *amen*?

Amen means "so be it!" It comes at the end of our prayer because we are confident that God keeps promises, and that nothing will separate us from the love of God, which endures forever.

THE 1883 CATECHISM

1. What is the chief end of man?

Man's chief end is to glorify God and to enjoy Him forever.

2. What rule has God given to direct us how we may glorify and enjoy Him?

The Word of God, which is contained in the Scriptures of the Old and the New Testament, is the only infallible rule to direct us how we may glorify and enjoy Him.

3. What do the Scriptures principally teach?

The Scriptures principally teach what man is to believe concerning God, and what duty God requires of man.

4. What is God?

God is a Spirit, infinite, eternal, and unchangeable in His being, wisdom, power, holiness, justice, goodness and truth.

5. Are there more gods than one?

There is one only, the living and true God.

6. How many persons are there in the Godhead?

There are three persons in the Godhead: the Father, the Son, and the Holy Spirit; and these three are one God, the same in substance, equal in power and glory.

7. What are the decrees of God?

The decrees of God are His wise and holy purposes to do what shall be for His glory. Sin not being for His glory, therefore, He has not decreed it.

8. How does God execute His decrees?

God executes His decrees in the works of creation, providence, and grace.

9. What is the work of creation?

The work of creation is God's making all things by the word of His power, and all very good.

10. How did God create man?

God created man, male and female, in uprightness and in His own image, endowed with all the attributes of moral agency.

11. What are God's works of providence?

God's works of providence are His preserving and so governing His creatures, and overruling their actions, as to manifest His wisdom, power, and goodness in promoting their welfare.

12. What special act of providence did God exercise toward man in the estate wherein he was created?

When God had created man, He entered into a covenant of life with him, upon condition of perfect obedience, forbidding him to eat of the tree of knowledge of good and evil, upon pain and death.

13. Did our first parents continue in the estate wherein they were created?

Our first parents, being left to the freedom of their own will, fell from the estate wherein they were created by sinning against God.

14. What is sin?

Sin is any want of conformity unto, or transgression of, the law of God.

15. What was the sin whereby our first parents fell from the estate wherein they were created?

The sin whereby our first prents fell from the estate wherein they were created was their disobeying God's command in eating the forbidden fruit.

16. What effect did Adam's sin have upon his posterity?

Adam's sin corrupted his moral nature and alienated him f rom God; and all mankind descending from him by ordinary generation inherit his corruption of nature, and become subject to sin and death.

17. Into what estate did the fall bring mankind?

The fall brought mankind into a state of alienation from God, which is spiritual death.

18. What does God require, that we may escape the punishment due for sin?

To escape the punishment due for sin, God requires of us repentance toward Him and faith in the Lord Jesus Christ.

19. What is repentance toward God?

Repentance toward God is that exercise whereby the sinner, out of a true sense of his guilt, with grief and hatred of sin, turns from it.

20. What is faith in Jesus Christ?

Faith in Jesus Christ, the ability of which is of grace, is receiving and resting upon Him alone for salvation as He is offered to us in the gospel.

21. What are the evils of that estate into which mankind fell?

Mankind, in consequence of the fall, have no communion with God, discern not spiritual things, prefer sin to holiness, suffer from the fear of death and remorse of conscience, and from the apprehension of future punishment.

22. Did God leave mankind to perish in this estate?

No; God out of His mere good pleasure and love, did provide salvation for all mankind.

23. How did God provide salvation for mankind?

By giving His Son, who became man, and so was and continues to be both God and man in one person, to be a propitiation for the sins of the world.

24. How did Christ, being the Son of God, become man?

Christ, the Son of God, became man by taking to himself a true body and a reasonable soul, being conceived by the power of the Holy Spirit, and born of the Virgin Mary, yet without sin.

25. What offices does Christ execute as our Redeemer?

Christ, as our Redeemer, executes the office of a prophet, of a priest, and of a king, both in His estate of humiliation and exaltation.

26. How does Christ execute the office of a prophet?

Christ executes the office of a prophet in revealing to us, by His Word and Spirit, the will of God for our salvation.

27. How does Christ execute the office of a priest?

Christ executes the office of a priest in having once offered Himself a sacrifice for sin, in reconciling us to God, and in making continual intercession for us.

28. How does Christ execute the office of a king?

Christ executes the office of a king in ruling and defending us, and in restraining and conquering all His and our enemies.

29. Wherein did Christ's humiliation consist?

Christ's humiliation consisted in His incarnation and the liabilities therewith connected, especially in His being made a sin offering for us, and in His death and burial.

30. Wherein consists Christ's exaltation?

Christ's exaltation consists in His resurrection from the dead on the third day, in ascending up into heaven, in sitting at the right hand of God, the Father, and in coming to judge the world at the last day.

31. How do we become partakers of the redemption provided by Christ?

We become partakers of the Redemption provided by Christ through the application of it to us by the Holy Spirit.

32. How does the Holy Spirit apply to us the Redemption provided by Christ?

The Holy Spirit applies to us the merits of Christ's death by taking of the things that are Christ's and showing them unto us, and thus enabling us to believe to the saving of our souls.

33.What is the work of the Holy Spirit?

The work of the Holy Spirit is to reprove the world of sin, of righteousness, and of judgment; to regenerate, comfort, and guide those who trust in Christ.

34. What benefits do those united to Christ derive from this union in this life?

Those who are united to Christ are justified, regenerated, adopted, sanctified, and enabled to grow in grace and in the knowledge of the truth.

35. What is *justification*?

Justification is an act of God's free grace, wherein He pardons all our sins, and accepts us as righteous in His sight, only for the righteousness of Christ imputed to us, and received by faith alone.

36. What is *regeneration*?

Regeneration is such renewing of the heart by the Holy Spirit as constitutes us new creatures in Christ, and enables us to love and enjoy God.

37. What is *adoption*?

Adoption is an act of God's free grace, whereby we are received into the number, and have a right to to all the privileges, of the sons of God.

38. What is growth in grace?

To grow in grace is to increase in the knowledge of spiritual things, to come to a deeper consciousness of our moral frailties and of our need of God's sustaining grace, by which alone we are enabled more faithfully to execute our vow of consecration, restrain our passions, and rejoice in the assurance that all things work together for our ultimate good.

39. What benefits do believers receive from Christ at their death?

The spirits of believers are, at death, freed from all temptation, all occasion of sin and suffering, and pass immediately into glory.

40. What benefits do believers receive from Christ at the resurrection?

At the resurrection the spirits of believers are clothed upon with spiritual and incorruptible bodies, fashioned like unto Christ's glorious body, and made perfectly blessed in the full enjoyment of God forever.

41. What does God require of man?

God requires of man obedience to His revealed will.

42. What rule of obedience did God reveal to man?

The moral law.

43. Wherein is the moral law summarily comprehended?

The moral law is summarily comprehended in the Ten Commandments.

44. What is the sum of the Ten Commandments?

The sum of the Ten Commandments is to love the Lord our God with all our mind and heart, and our neighbor as ourselves.

45. What is the preface to the Ten Commandments?

The preface to the Ten Commandments is in these words: "I am the Lord thy God, which have brought thee out of the land of Egypt, out of the house of bondage."

46. What does the preface to the Ten Commandments teach?

The preface to the Ten Commandments teaches that because God is the Lord, and our God and Redeemer, therefore we are bound to keep all His commandments.

47. Which is the first commandment?

The first commandment is, Thou shalt have no other gods before me.

48. What is required of the first commandment?

The first commandment requires us to acknowledge and worship the true God only.

49. What is forbidden in the first commandment?

The first commandment forbids the worship of any other than the true God.

50. What is specially taught by the words, "Before me", in the first commandment?

The words, "before me," in the first commandment, teach that God is much displeased with the sin of having any other god.

51. Which is the second commandment?

The second commandment is, Thou shalt not make unto thee any graven image, or any likeness of any thing which is in heaven above, or that is in the earth beneath, or that is in the water under the earth. Thou shalt not bow down thyself to them, nor serve them; for I the Lord thy God am a jealous God, visiting the iniquity of the fathers upon the children unto the third and fourth generation of them that hate me; and showing mercy unto thousands of them that love Me, and keep My commandments.

52. What is required in the second commandment?

The second commandment requires that the the worship of God shall be maintained in simplicity and purity.

53. What is forbidden in the second commandment?

The second commandment forbids the worshiping of God by images, or in any other way not appointed in His Word.

54. What are the reasons annexed to the second commandment?

The reasons annexed to the second commandment are, God's sovereignty over us, His property in us, and His zeal for His own worship.

55. What is the third commandment?

The third commandment is, Thou shalt not take the name of the

Lord thy God in vain: for the Lord will not hold him guiltless that taketh His name in vain.

56. What is required in the third commandment?

The third commandment requires the holy and reverent use of God's name.

57. What is forbidden in the third commandment?

The third commandment forbids all profanity or improper use of God's name.

58. What is the reason annexed to the third commandment?

The reason annexed to the third commandment is, that however the breakers of this commandment may escape punishment from men, yet the Lord our God will not suffer them to escape His righteous judgment.

59. Which is the fourth commandment?

The fourth commandment is, Remember the Sabbath day to keep it holy. Six days shalt thou labor, and do all thy work: but the seventh day is the Sabbath of the Lord thy God: in it thou shalt not do any work, thou, nor thy son, nor thy daughter, thy manservant, nor thy maidservant, nor thy cattle, nor thy stranger that is within thy gates: for in six days the Lord made heaven and earth, the sea, and all that in them is, and rested the seventh day: wherefore the Lord blessed the Sabbath day, and hallowed it.

60. What is required in the fourth commandment?

The fourth commandment requires one day out of seven to be kept as a holy Sabbath unto God.

61.Which day of the seven had God appointed to be the Sabbath?

God has been pleased to appoint one day in seven to be kept holy unto Him, which, from the beginning of the world to the resurrection of Christ, was the last day of the week; and, after the resurrection of Christ was changed unto the first day of the week, which, in the Scriptures, is called the Lord's Day.

62. How is the Sabbath to be sanctified?

The Sabbath is to be sactified by resting from employments and recreations of a secular character, by the public and private worship of God, and by works of necessity and mercy.

63. What is forbidden in the fourth commandment?

The fourth commandment forbids the omission or careless performance of the duties required, and the profanation of the day by idleness, or by unnecessary thoughts, words, or works, about our worldly employments and recreations.

64. What are the reasons annexed to the fourth commandment?

The reasons annexed to the fourth commandment are God's setting apart six days of the week for our own employments, His designating the seventh as the Sabbath of the Lord, His own example, and His blessing the Sabbath day.

65. Which is the fifth commandment?

The fifth commandment is, Honor thy father and thy mother: that thy days may be long upon the land which the Lord thy God giveth thee.

66. What is required in the fifth commandment?

The fifth commandment requires children to honor their parents, and to obey them in all things lawful.

67. What is forbidden in the fifth commandment?

The fifth commandment forbids all kinds of dishonor and disobedience, in things lawful, toward parents.

68. What is the reason annexed to the fifth commandment?

The reason annexed to the fifth commandment is a promise of long life and prosperity, as far as it shall serve for God's glory and their own good, to all such as keep this commandment.

69. What is the sixth commandment?

The sixth commandment is, Thou shalt not kill.

70. What is required in the sixth commandment?

The sixth commandment requires all lawful endeavors to preserve our own life and the life of others.

71. What is forbidden in the sixth commandment?

The sixth commandment forbids the taking away of our own life, or the life of another, unlawfully, or whatsoever tends thereunto.

72. Which is the seventh commandment?

The seventh commandment is, Thou shalt not commit adultery.

73. What is required in the seventh commandment?

The seventh commandment requires chastity in desires and actions.

74. What is forbidden in the seventh commandment?

The seventh commandment forbids all unchaste desires and actions.

75. Which is the eighth commandment?

The eighth commandment is, Thou shalt not steal.

76. What is required in the eighth commandment?

The eighth commandment requires honesty in all our dealings with, and conduct toward, others in regard to property.

77. What is forbidden in the eighth commandment?

The eighth commandment forbids the taking by stealth, or by force, or by misrepresentation, what justly belongs to another.

78. Which is the ninth commandment?

The ninth commandment is, Thou shalt not bear false witness against thy neighbor.

79. What is required in the ninth commandment?

The ninth commandment requires a conscientious regard to truth in reference to others.

80. What is forbidden in the ninth commandment?

The ninth commandment forbids whatever varies from the truth, or conceals it, or is injurious to the good name or rights of another.

81.Which is the tenth commandment?

The tenth commandment is, Thou shalt not covet thy neighbor's house, thou shalt not covet thy neighbor's wife, nor his manservant, nor his maidservant, nor his ox, nor his ass, nor anything that is thy neighbor's.

82. What is required in the tenth commandment?

The tenth commandment requires contentment with our own condition, with a right and charitable frame of spirit toward another, and all that is his.

83. What is forbidden in the tenth commandment?

The tenth commandment forbids all discontentment with our own estate, envying or grieving at the good of another, and all inordinate motions or affections to any thing that is his.

84. Is any man perfectly able to keep the moral law?

No.

85. Are all transgressions of the law equally heinous?

Some sins in themselves, and by reason of the several aggravations, are more heinous in the sight of God than others.

86. What does every sin deserve?

Every sin, being an offense against God, deserves His displeasure, and subjects the sinner thereto.

87. What are the outward and ordinary means whereby Christ communicates to us the benefits of redemption?

The outward and ordinary means whereby Christ communicates to us the benefits of redemption are His ordinances, especially the Word, sacraments and prayer.

88. How is the Word made effectual to salvation?

The Holy Spirit makes the reading, and especially the preaching, of the Word an effectual means of convincing and converting sinners, and of building them up in holiness and comfort through faith unto salvation.

89. How is the Word to be read and heard, that it may become effectual unto salvation?

That the Word may become effectual unto salvation, we must attend thereunto with diligence, preparation, and prayer; receive it with faith and love, lay it up in our hearts, and practice it in our lives.

90. How do the sacraments become effectual means of growth in grace to believers?

The sacraments become effectual means of growth in grace, not from any virtue in them, or in him who administers them, but only by the blessing of Christ, and the working of the Holy Spirit in those who by faith receive them.

91. What is a sacrament?

A sacrament is a holy ordinance instituted by Christ, wherein, by sensible signs, He and the benefits of the new covenant are symbolized.

92. What are the sacraments of the New Testament?

The sacraments of the New Testament are Baptism and the Lord's Supper.

93. What is baptism?

Water baptism is sacrament administered in the name of the Trinity, is symbolic of regeneration, is the seal of the Covenant of Grace, and with adults, is declarative of a purpose to live according to God's word.

94. To whom is baptism to be administered?

Baptism is to be administered to believers and their infant children.

95. What is the Lord's Supper?

The Lord's Supper is a sacrament instituted by Christ, and is commemorative of His death, in the celebration of which the communicant declares His faith in Christ as a crucified, risen, and ascended Savior, who will return again without sin unto salvation.

96. What is required of those who partake of the Lord's Supper?

Those who partake of the Lord's Supper are required to examine themselves as to whether Christ dwells in them by faith, enabling them spiritually to discern His body.

97. What is prayer?

Prayer is an offering up of our desires unto God, for things agreeable to His will, in the name of Christ, with confession of our sins, and thankful acknowledgment of His mercies.

98. What rule has God given for our direction in prayer?

The whole Word of God is of use to direct us in prayer, but the special rule of direction is that form of prayer which Christ taught His disciples, commonly called the Lord's Prayer.

99. What does the preface of the Lord's Prayer teach us?

The preface of the Lord's Prayer—which is, Our Father which art in heaven—teaches us to draw near to God with holy reverence and confidence, as children to a father able and ready to help us, and that we should pray with and for others.

100. For what do we pray in the first petition?

In the first petition—which is, Hallowed be thy name—we pray that God would enable us and others to always think and speak of His name with the deepest reverence.

101. For what do we pray in the second petition?

In the second petition, which is Thy kingdom come—we pray that Satan's kingdom may be destroyed, and that the kingdom of grace may be advanced, ourselves and others brought into it, and kept in it, and that the kingdom of glory may be hastened.

102. For what do we pray in the third petition?

In the third petition, which is Thy will be done in earth, as it is in heaven—we pray that God, by His grace would make us able and willing to know, obey, and submit to His will in all things, as the angels do in heaven.

103. For what do we pray in the fourth petition?

In the fourth petition, which is, Give us this day our daily bread—-we pray that God's free gift we may receive a competent portion of the good things of life, and enjoy His blessing with them.

30 THE CATECHISM (1883)

104. For what do we pray in the fifth petition?

In the fifth petition—which is, And forgive us our debts, as we forgive our debtors—we pray that God, for Christ's sake, would freely pardon all our sins; which we are the rather encouraged to ask, because by His grace we are enabled from the heart to forgive others.

105. For what do we pray in the sixth petition?

In the sixth petition—which is, And lead us not into temptation, but deliver us from evil—we pray that God would either keep us from being tempted to sin, or support and deliver us when we are tempted.

OTHER RESOURCES

As you study the *Catechism for Cumberland Presbyterians* and the *Confession of Faith* you may find the following resources useful.

Confession of Faith and Government of the Cumberland Presbyterian Church/Cumberland Presbyterian Church in America 1984 (Memphis, Tennessee: Office of the General Assembly of the Cumberland Presbyterian Church, August 2010).

Morrow, Hubert, *Covenant of Grace: A Thread Through Scripture* (Memphis, Tennessee: Board of Christian Education of the Cumberland Presbyterian Church, 1996).

Confession of Faith and Government of the Cumberland Presbyterian Church (Revised 1883) (Frontier Press, Memphis, Tennessee: 1985).

Reagin, Ewell K., *What Cumberland Presbyterians Believe (Revised)* (Historical Foundation of the Cumberland Presbyterian Church and the Cumberland Presbyterian Church in America: Memphis, Tennessee, March 2011).

Catechism for the Cumberland Presbyterian Church with Study Guide (Discipleship Ministry Team of the Ministry Council of the Cumberland Presbyterian Church: Memphis, Tennessee, Spring 2012).

Campbell, Thomas D., & Anna N. Bolling, *A Study Guide for Use with the Confession of Faith for Cumberland Presbyterians* (Discipleship Ministry Team of the Ministry Council of the Cumberland Presbyterian Church: Memphis, Tennessee, December 2011).

Made in the USA
Charleston, SC
27 May 2012